Option Income Strategy

1st edition by

Tradesignalgo

Option Income Strategy

Copyright © 2019 TradeSignAlgo

All rights reserved.

ISBN:

DEDICATION

Wealth gained hastily will dwindle, but whoever gathers little by little will increase it. (Proverbs 13:11 ESV). Many people pursue wealth hoping to strike the largest of fortune in the shortest of time. They follow all kinds of strategies looking for big payouts such as buying options to bet on the big crash or rally, engage in highly leveraged directional trading for big gains without considering the equivalent losses that wipe out their accounts. It took me a couple of years to realize risk, reward and probability goes together like the holy trinity. The foundations of this book is based on the concept of quantitative validation, not by gut feel or experience. Here is a quote from the greatest investor of all time.

"The quantitative factors lend themselves far better to thoroughgoing analysis than do the qualitative factors. The former are fewer in number, more easily obtainable, and much better suited to the forming of definite and dependable conclusions."
— **Benjamin Graham**

CONTENTS

DEDICATION

FOREWORD

1 50/50 CHANCE

2 THE PRINCIPLE

3 WINNING 67%

4 TRADE SETUP

5 VALIDATING

6 LIVE WALK FORWARDS

7 TOOLS OF THE TRADE

8 PITFALLS TO AVOID

ABOUT THE AUTHOR

OTHER MATERIALS BY AUTHOR

FOREWORD

This book is dedicated to the countless souls in their quest for financial freedom, and the pain and disappointment endured through the countless time and money by unscrupulous vendors and fake trading experts. Many are lured by promises of vast fortunes and paid thousands of dollars for courses that all amount to nothing in the end. Teaching you to trade, they say, but all you have gotten are vague rules and indicators that works temporarily, until the next upgrade to improved formula, at another expense cost.

This book will show you the exact rules to follow, you can scrutinize them and results will be readily available on the Internet for your analysis. You do not need complex understanding of option Greeks and methodology, just a simple and logical risk and reward allocation for your trade set up. There will be no lengthy words and complex jargon to confuse you, I will spare you this pain. By the time you finish this book, of which you can complete within half a day, and understand the principle and precise calculation for your course of action, you will know exactly what to look for to generate monthly income from option selling.

Option selling is not without risks, the fact is that it could potentially blow up your account if you do not manage it. Fortunately there are workarounds to limit this downside risk. The method here does not advocate naked option selling, but using a risk hedging method to limit the downside exposure when things go terribly wrong. Why only downside exposure and not upside? We will explain as you read on.

Options is the only method to structure your win and loss amounts into absolute numbers. Without options, each potential winning or losing trade can go beyond any historical expectancy you can imagine. Just like the banker at the casino, if you can limit the wins and losses at each hand, and play it with a probability, you can come out ahead with many rounds. Of course there are some who have chosen to ignore this risk structure, and many have ended up to the demise of their trading career. Options if sold naked can truly destroy your trading account, be warned. Follow the methods in this book and you will avoid that destruction.

1 50/50 CHANCE

Just place your bet on UP or DOWN, loss you double up, WIN you take a profit and quit the game. Easy formula to win in financial markets isn't it? Not so straight forward, win/loss payouts are not fixed constants especially if you are betting on the next bullish or bearish move. Each move can be larger or smaller than expected since the magnitude of each move are not linear. Therefore you cannot take the expectancy of fixed payouts like the casino and apply it to the financial markets (stocks and shares, forex and gold). To come out ahead is not a point in time, but continuous journey. You must be prepared to walk the journey into eternity and prepare your arsenal of resource in monetary funds.

The appeal of 'cracking' the financial code has baffled many wise men, academics, adventurers, risk takers, engineers, scientists, mathematicians and even simple folks. Many have left with losses in vain. This financial game is harder to beat than your usual game of chess. If you wish to take it as a full time income job, then you need to raise the stakes by 10 times. Minimum capital of $100,000 and expected return of 2% a month, with a risk tolerance of 10%. Without this amount of capital to start, I suggest you stop reading right now and come back when you have that spare capital. If you can mentally withstand that kind of drawdowns, I have a consistent method to show you exactly how to do it. The best part is, you get to play it with time advantage in your hands. The longer the time passed, the better your advantage. Option selling gives you the income through the premium collected and that ages well with time decay. Because selling an option entails unlimited risk, we will have to mitigate that risk through structures using vertical spreads.

2 THE PRINCIPLE

Unlike most option strategies which are derived from complex technical studies and complicated Greeks such as delta, vega, theta, the methodology shown in this book is backed by quantitative sound logical strategies of the fundamental behaviour of equity markets. Consider this, the directional bias of the stock markets as a whole has been positive over time, due to organic growth and profit generated. More so if you go for the top basket of corporate performers. If you look at the major stock index performance in the last 100 years, all have risen in value over time. FTSE100, German DAX30, America Dow Jones 30, S&P500, Japan Nikkei 225, etc. With the most extensive history available, is Dow Jone 30 with data for the past 100 years.

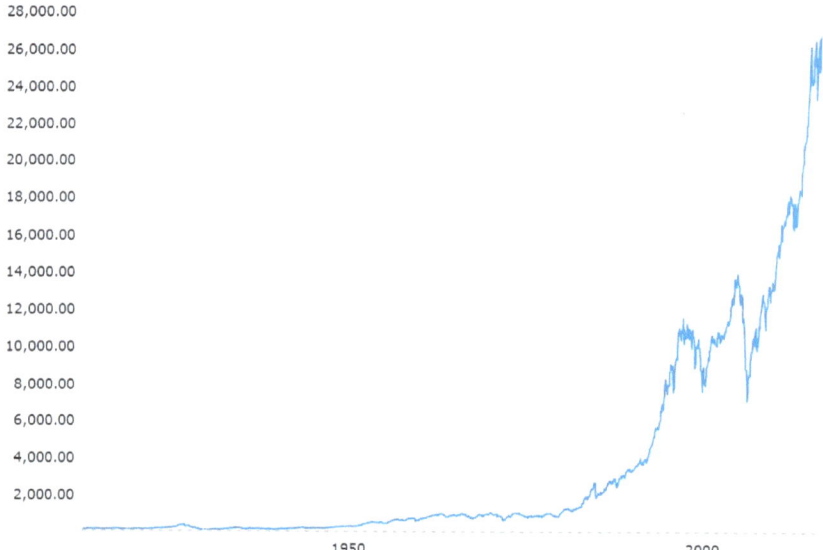

Figure 2.1 https://www.macrotrends.net/1319/dow-jones-100-year-historical-chart

If we consider the most diversified basket of companies amongst this list, we can zero in on the Standard and Poors 500 index. Below is a chart showing the monthly performance of last 90 years from 1930 - 2019. What does it tell us? Fundamentally, prices tend to rise due to creation of value and services being consumed and monetary resources being invested.

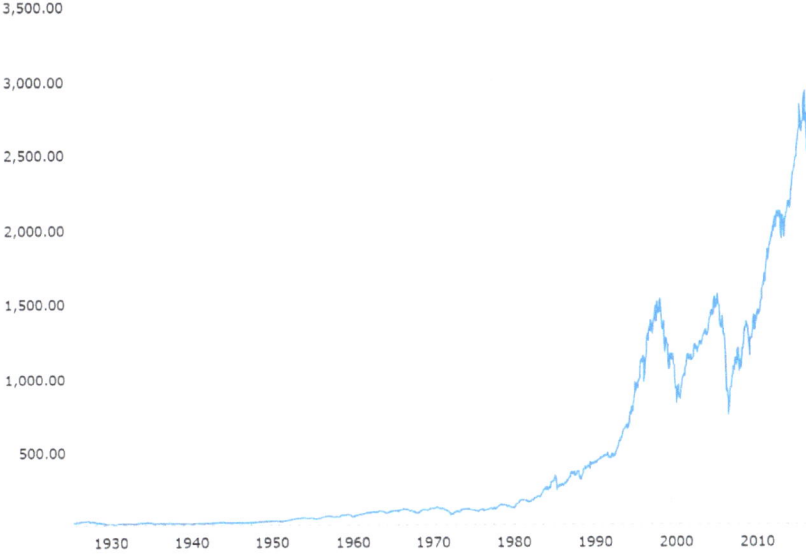

Figure 2.2
https://www.macrotrends.net/2324/sp-500-historical-chart-data

Japan has a shorter economic history than US, nevertheless, their 67 year historical chart is pretty impressive too. Below is a log scale of the chart adjusted for inflation.

Figure 2.3
https://www.macrotrends.net/2593/nikkei-225-index-historical-chart-data

Below chart shows the leading country in Europe, German DAX 30, again it is positive skew in the long term.

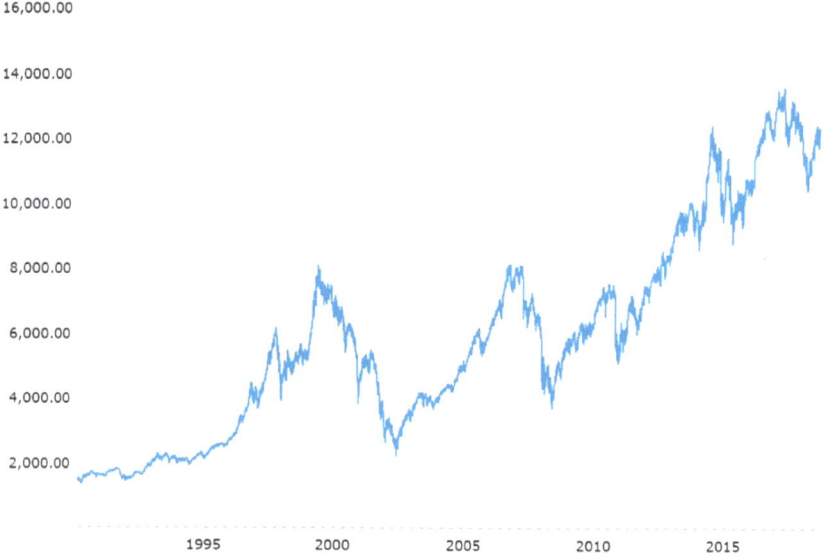

Figure 2.4
https://www.macrotrends.net/2595/dax-30-index-germany-historical-chart-data

With the upward bias of the equity indices over the long term, it makes sense to trade on the side of long rather than picking the tops. Sure, picking shorts and occasionally may give you the adrenalin flow when you are right, but most of the time you will be suffering losses before you hit that jackpot. In my other book "5 Simple Strategies for Complex Markets", I have backtested a long only equity through seasonal days of the month with only a single bullish filter mechanism. The rules are easy to follow, between 25th to 31st of the month, if the previous day price close below the open and closing price is still above the 200 day moving average of daily closes, initiate a buy at the market open. Hold it for 3 weeks and exit on the 19th day of the month. Repeat on the 25th of next cycle.

Using this rule we can structure an option selling strategy that capitalizes on market bull cycles as well as flat cycles, allying with time on our side. The only downside risk is when market crashes down to which the option spread comes critical. This is only 33% (⅓) chance of loss, out of the market scenarios of up, down, flat.

How then do we structure the option trades, what level of strikes and how far the strikes for the spreads? Let us explore that in the next chapter.

3 WINNING 67%

Since the probability of loss in case the market tanked is 33%, the chance of a profit is 67% ! How then the strikes should be chosen? We need to choose the level where most liquidity and volume is traded and yet far enough away from current market price. The ideal level would be to choose near delta 0.3 or 67% probability of in-the-money strike level. How about the expiration date, for that you choose one that corresponds as close to Friday on the 3rd week of the month as near to 19th day of the month. Now taking the example of S&P 500 index, which contract and exchange should we choose. Reckon that this index and its derivatives can be traded on CME as options on index futures, CBOE as index options and AMEX as options on ETF. Fret not as I promised this book to be written as simple to understand as possible. No mental bombardment of complex statistics and formulas. Life is complex as it is, we do not need to complicate our lives further. We have structure a solution combining basic outright quantitative trading foundation into a viable option income generation process. If you still cannot believe trading options can be so easy, read on to find out the exact methodology to follow. Next Chapter will focus on the exact setup method to execute this strategy.

4 TRADE SETUP

What you need are simple and free tools that you can use. On your browser, navigate to CBOE.com. We are going to make use of the options on CBOE because of one important point, the options are cash settled and marked to market on expiration day. That makes things really simple, you just settle the profit and loss marked to the settlement price of index, no need to take delivery and run the risk of an outright position upon expiry. For assignment, it is also marked to market and settled in cash. Another advantage of trading the SPX options on CBOE is being European style, you do not have to worry about early assignment. Everything is cash settled on the expiration day, making it very easy to monitor.

Option Income Strategy

Let us go the option chain to get the list of quotes. http://www.cboe.com/delayedquote/quote-table?ticker=SPX or if you have an account with TD Ameritrade, their excellent ThinkorSwim platform will show the same information in real time.

Step 1 From the 25th of the month till 31st, check the previous day closing price if it is below the opening price. Check also it is above the 200 day moving average of all daily closing prices. This can easily be done using freeware such as TradingView or Investing.com. If both are true, then navigate to the expiration date nearest to 19th of the following month. In this case today's date is 25th June, so zoom in to the 19th July expiration.

Figure 4.1

13

Option Income Strategy

Figure 4.2

Step 2 Once you have zoomed in to the delta that is -0.30 on the Put option, go to the corresponding Strike which in this case is SPX 2940 or SPXW 2940. The latter is the Weekly options, you may choose the SPX monthly options since the Int (Open Interest) is higher. Next choose the Strike level for your risk-off spread, you can have a choice from a minimum of 5 points, 10 points, 15 points or even wider than that. Of course the dynamics are different, wider spread gives you greater probability of getting it correct but each wrong outcome will set you back by the equivalent drawdown. And the period to recover from drawdown will increase with wider spread points. Not to mention the liquidity of the different strike levels. There is also the mental psychology of going through that drawdown, you will need to understand this in advance. A simple way is to choose 10 points away from your main Put strike, 2940-10 = 2930 Put. This represents 10*100(multiplier) = USD1000 of maximum possible loss (excluding commission) on this spread. See contract specifications below

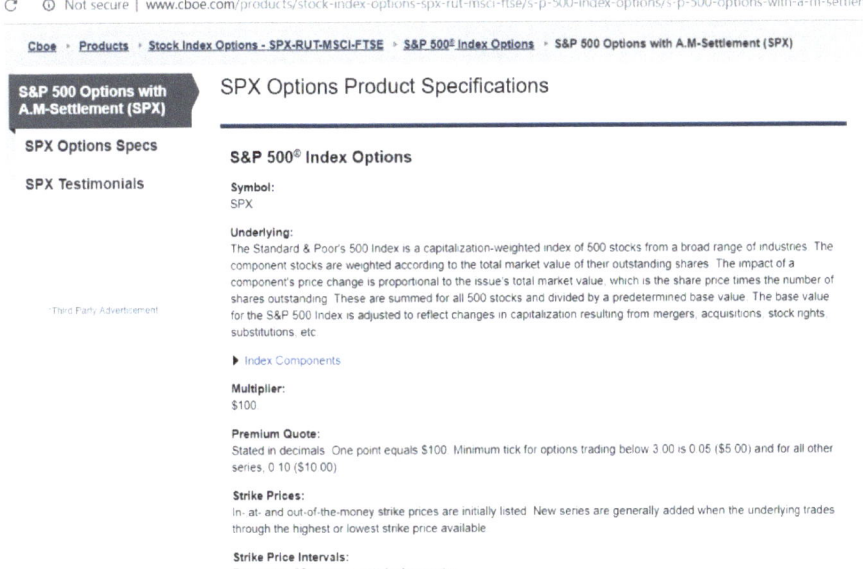

Figure 4.3

Based on the Last price in figure 4.1, the 2940P vs 2930P is 13.30 vs 11.45 based on last traded. Based on Bid/Ask, 2940P @ 11.5/12 vs 2930P @ 9.8/10.2, you can try to leg a sell Credit Put Spread 2940P/2930P @ 12.2/10.2 for credit of 2 points. That will give you $200 before commissions in option premium while ensuring your maximum loss at $1000 - $200 = $800 excluding commissions. This setup will correspond to 67% chance of success holding to expiry.

If you use ThinkorSwim (ToS) platform (https://www.thinkorswim.com/platform/index.html), the software even allows you to place a combo set of vertical spread orders to work on their server, without you having to fill the orders manually separately. There are many other good software such as TradeStation, Interactive Brokers TWS, NinjaTrader, OEC Trader and MultiCharts that allow you to submit the spread order as a single trade combination. As an added advantage, you can also choose to liquidate the positions earlier should the market rally strongly. Otherwise, there is no need for further trade adjustments, this method has a natural stop loss component built into the strategy by the spread differential in the strike price, you do not need to put any stop loss order.

Below is the interface using ToS, S&P 500 index rallied to an all time high yesterday night to 2995.82 close from 2973.01 previous close, one day after the screenshot on CBOE taken yesterday. You will notice the Put deltas and probability goes lower/further from the market level as it rallies, an inverse relationship of Put options.

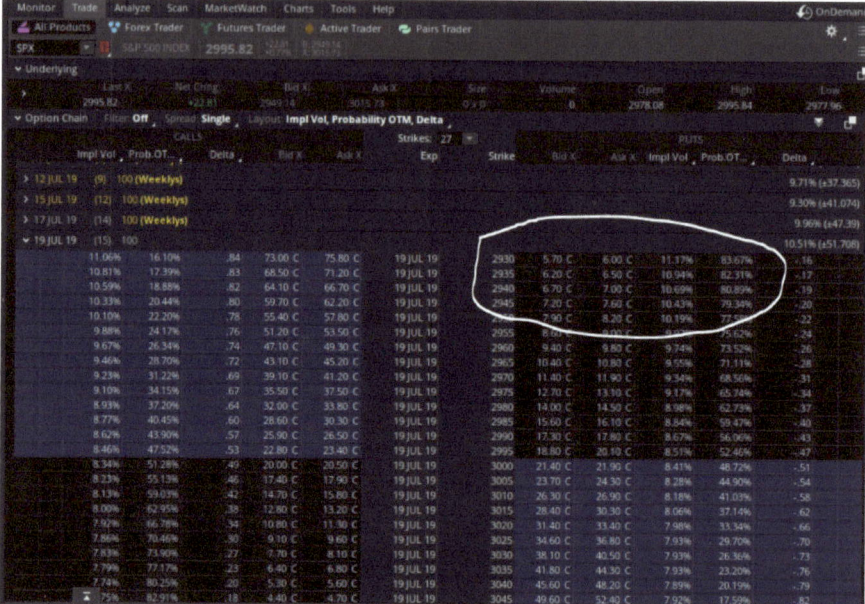

Figure 4.4

The ToS allows you to place the vertical spread order directly as a customized combo, convenience of spread execution.

Option Income Strategy

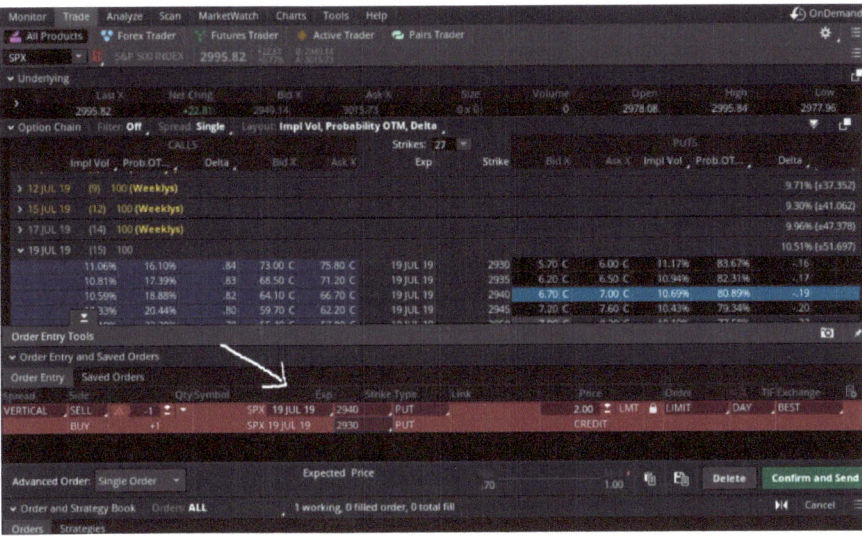

Figure 4.5

For reference, below is the CBOE price format, delta for SPX 2930/2940 is -0.1631/-0.1852 respectively. ToS shows -0.16 / -0.19 respectively (Figure 4.4)

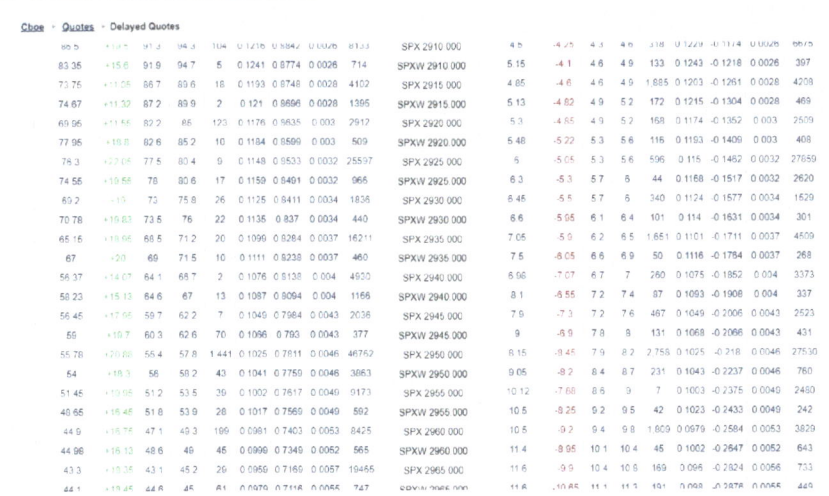

5 VALIDATING

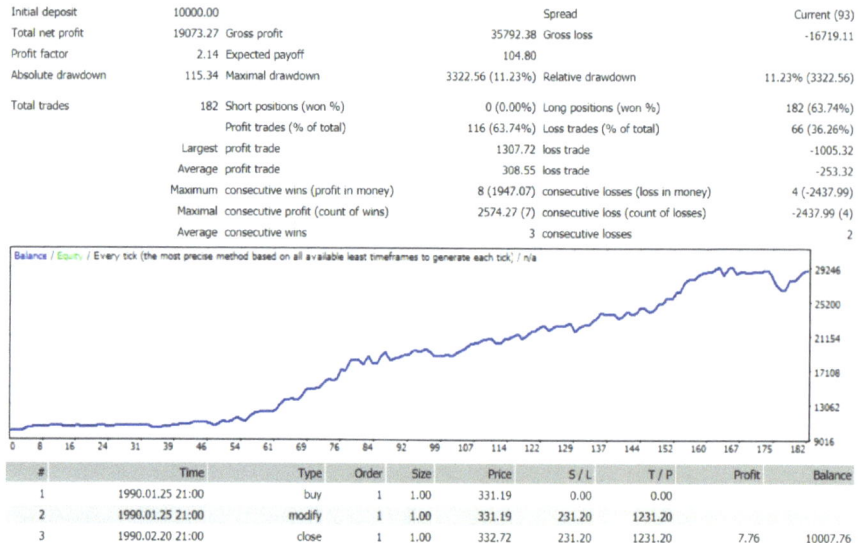

Figure 5.1

The long-only strategy was back-tested on MT4 running data from 1990 to 2017 using the entry conditions in Chapter 4 and with a hard stop of 100 points. For the benefit of doubt, there are summarized as below again.

Entry Condition: From 25th of the month, check yesterday market close price is above 200 day moving average close and it is below yesterday open price. Using the Put option strikes expiring near the 19th day of the following month, sell the Put Strike at -0.3 delta and buy the Put at the next higher Strike up at 10 points away. Hold it till expiry. CBOE SPX is recommended as the options are cash settled. That's it, no complicated Greeks and volatility studies to confuse you. Essentially, this is using options to trade the directional bias of the equity markets over the long term. Do this every month end and you will generate a stream of option selling income. Selling a minimum of 1 lot spread will give you income of USD200 in premium on the SPX with maximum risk of USD800 loss if your strike difference is 10 points wide. Online brokers charge a minimal commission of USD3.95 per side, so you can look to pay about USD7.90 to leg up this spread. Some offer promotions of zero fees if you let it expire worthless. Even by liquidating earlier a transaction of USD15.8 is still decent for newbie trader. You can build your volume and negotiate for even lower rates when you build up your base. Check out TDAmeritrade or Interactive Brokers or TastyTrades for their online rates.

6 LIVE WALK FORWARDS

Below is a screenshot for actual trades executed via ToS in 2018.

Exec Time	Spread	Side	Qty-Pos Effect	Symbol	Exp	Strike	Type	Price	Net Price	Order Type
10/9/18 02:02:50	VERTICAL	BUY	+1 TO CLOSE	SPX	19 OCT 18	2850	PUT	19.58	2.45	STPLMT
		SELL	-1 TO CLOSE	SPX	19 OCT 18	2840	PUT	17.13		DEBIT
10/8/18 21:30:05	VERTICAL	SELL	-1 TO OPEN	SPX	19 OCT 18	2850	PUT	19.60	2.30	LMT
		BUY	+1 TO OPEN	SPX	19 OCT 18	2840	PUT	17.30		CREDIT
10/6/18 04:00:00	VERTICAL	BUY	+1 TO CLOSE	SPX	19 OCT 18	2890	PUT	28.28	3.55	STPLMT
		SELL	-1 TO CLOSE	SPX	19 OCT 18	2880	PUT	24.73		DEBIT
9/25/18 22:59:03	VERTICAL	SELL	-1 TO OPEN	SPX	19 OCT 18	2890	PUT	17.40	2.00	LMT
		BUY	+1 TO OPEN	SPX	19 OCT 18	2880	PUT	15.40		CREDIT
7/13/18 00:03:18	VERTICAL	BUY	+1 TO CLOSE	SPX	20 JUL 18	2660	PUT	.80	.10	LMT
		SELL	-1 TO CLOSE	SPX	20 JUL 18	2650	PUT	.70		DEBIT
6/28/18 01:17:56	VERTICAL	SELL	-1 TO OPEN	SPX	20 JUL 18	2660	PUT	22.00	1.90	LMT
		BUY	+1 TO OPEN	SPX	20 JUL 18	2650	PUT	20.10		CREDIT
6/12/18 23:51:35	VERTICAL	BUY	+1 TO CLOSE	SPX	22 JUN 18	2660	PUT	1.85	.20	LMT
		SELL	-1 TO CLOSE	SPX	22 JUN 18	2650	PUT	1.65		DEBIT

Figure 6.1

As you can see, you could get better entry price than 2.00 or even 2.30 depending on the volatility of the market. The ToS platform also allows setting of StopLoss on your open position even before the expiry date. This however is not recommended as you can get stopped out by the volatility while the market recovers to normalized levels in your favour. The SPX options are European style in nature, so it does not run the risk of early assignment anyway.

7 TOOLS OF THE TRADE

As starters to the trading game, we all want to keep our costs low. Fortunately with the internet, we can get access to these tools for free. Market data charged by regulated exchanges are costly but it can be gotten for free as a retail trader.

For the moving average indicator, you can get it easily from TradingView or Investing.com for free. ToS also provides most of the charts and data for free for retail clients.

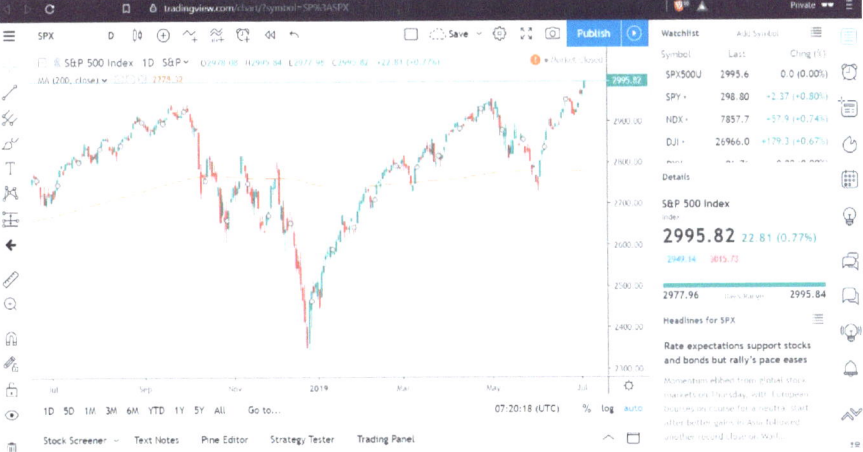

Figure 7.1

To generate trade setups, you do not need complicated steps and processes, that will only cause confusion. The methods described are designed to keep things as simple to understand as possible.

8 PITFALLS TO AVOID

Always enter the position only after the market closed lower on the previous day, reason being that will give you an advantage as the Puts will be priced higher. E.g. Puts are more valuable in premium when markets go down. Never use market order to enter the positions, especially in option market, the spread can be wider than usual, so choose the mid point price and enter using a Limit order. Of course you could end up without a position being triggered, that is the risk you must take, lost of opportunity. Never be greedy. Avoid hysterical about the position, once orders are filled, check for the positions and do not keep tracking the positions every minute. Never let the news or media affect your trading decision, the best is to shut them off, if news are so reliable in trading, all journalists and news analyst would be millionaires by now.

ABOUT THE AUTHOR

With over 20 years of experience in the financial industry since 1997 from operations to front line trading floor and technology specialist in algorithmic trading and direct market access. I hope to educate new traders seeking to approach the financial markets as a potential avenue to grow and increase their net worth. Programming is not as daunting as you perceived, I have picked it up through self learning, you can do it too and that is part of the reason for this material.

With full time professional floor trader experience on the mechanics of open outcry market place, and graduated with a Bachelor in Business and Finance from the University of Portsmouth with Finance background, the crossroads of trading and finance is molded into a unique synergy. I have witnessed the transition of open outcry floor trading to electronic trading, how it serves to fuel the growth of electronic trading tools (PATS, TT, GL, Proprietary software) which are good tools to trade. (I have hands on experience with each of them). But you need to have the concept right and know which tool is suitable for your strategy. No matter how advanced a front end trading interface provides, it is a simple methods that work.

For retail traders, it is relatively easy to explore algorithmic trading with Metatrader 4/5 MQL programming, This is a good start for those without programming background. Advance users with developer background can try Python, but that requires a lot of built from the ground up. To prove that quantitative and automatic trading is sustainable for the long term, I have established TradeSignalgo as an experimental algorithmic based automated strategy in 2008. Developed and forward tested trading models from 2008 to 2013. Thankfully automation is still surviving and running a portfolio of strategies live since 2013 on MT4 on Forex and CFDs. After having traded a proprietary account for quantitative strategies in futures, market neutral arbitrage and options, I can deduce that you do not need powerful computers to get returns.

For those sceptics, you can monitor my live trading via Twitter. Follow my Twitter for daily live trade signals Automated Trading @Algo_Signals. A few books on trading strategies including source codes are available on Amazon if you guys are interested in a quick start to Algo path. The templates will help you get a head start, that was how it helped me to take off. To be a good programmer you do not need to write from scratch, the best developers copy from what others have built and customize to their own taste. The templates I have are free for your own use and modification, just be kind enough to give credits when you find them useful. They are original and not taken off any copyrights or patents.

OTHER MATERIALS BY AUTHOR

Here is the link to the book list

https://www.amazon.com/s?k=tradesignalgo&rh=n%3A154606011&ref=nb_sb_noss

This book explains how simple methods can be applied to the finance world to navigate your financial goals, from passive to active strategies you can deploy. As financial products grow more and more, keeping these 5 simple strategies will allow you to filter out the unnecessary noise and focus on what works. This is The Book to go for if you have limited time for managing your investments.

Forex trading has challenged many intellects and offers many opportunities for those looking to profit from it. However many systems and strategies developed are short in lifespan, spectacular results within a short time and blow out in less than 2 years. The algorithm highlighted in this book shows a live trading strategy since 2013 and still surviving in the markets. Bonus source codes give you the freedom to adapt and modify further the concepts of the strategy with detailed description of the entry and exit rules.

This book will contain the exact trade details of the long-only equity strategy on the S&P 500 index for those interested to investigate the back test results. That will give you the confidence of the underlying principle of this Short Put Vertical spread strategy outlined in this book. You can use the source code to trade the outright CFD index or modify it to your own preference.

www.ingramcontent.com/pod-product-compliance
Lightning Source LLC
Chambersburg PA
CBHW040306220526
45473CB00002B/595